RIPENING

Richard Hague

RIPENING

POEMS BY RICHARD HAGUE

To Brian, years after the first madnesses that
started all this.

Best to you,

Dick

OHIO STATE UNIVERSITY PRESS
COLUMBUS

Library of Congress Cataloging in Publication Data

Hague, Richard, 1947–
  Ripening

  I. Title.
PS2558.A32345E5 1983   811'.54   83-19414
ISBN 0-8142-0354-X

To My Parents

CONTENTS

ACKNOWLEDGMENTS

Acknowledgment is gratefully made for permission to reprint poems in *Ripening* that appeared earlier in the following magazines and journals: *Adena*: "In the Woods beyond the Coal Fields," "Hounds," "Moths above the Fire," "One for Annie"; *Appalachian Heritage*: "Fire in Steubenville," "Country Matters"; *Cincinnati Poetry Review*: "What to Watch for in the Country"; *Hiram Poetry Review*: "Sparrows Drinking"; *Laurel Review*: "Cures"; *Live Writers*: "Going Back the Hard Way"; *Ohio Journal*: "Women on Porches outside Hannibal, Ohio," "Where I Come From There Are Woman Weeping," "An Unsent Letter of Darwin's," "Night," "Night Stop at the Crossroads," "Moose Ridge Apple Wine"; *Open Places*: "Horse Carcass," "Snag"; *Sackbut Review*: "Coming Out of Ice"; *Vegetable Box*: "October." Several of these poems previously have appeared in *Crossings*, an anthology published by the Cincinnati Area Poetry Press under a grant from the Ohio Arts Council.

I *❧* FOUNDING THE WORLD

Religious man has always sought
to fix his abode at 'the center of
the world.' If the world is to be
believed in, it must be *founded*.

—Mircea Eliade,
The Sacred And The Profane

GOING BACK THE HARD WAY

1

We stand in the center
of a field
whose edges are lost
in mist.
From the ghost of air
comes the sound of a man
driving long nails in a coffin.
Then it is gone.

Back on the road,
the world rebuilds
as sun burns off thick fog.
The Burma-Shave signs,
dim stations of the cross,
disappear around a bony ridge of skull.

2

The only crucifixion known of
in these parts
involved a black man
from Wellsburg, West Virginia.
They hoisted him kicking
up a skinned pole
on a morning much like this,
in 1892.
Fathers brought their sons,
as a lesson,

3

and made them touch the body
when they dumped it in a wagon.

3

The Sunday paper
scatters on the porch's spattered floor.
We are not likely to pick it up,
to rearrange its pages as we used to.

4

We close the door, feeling
splintery wood rasp at our spines,
the long tongue of paralysis.
All day, a numbness spreads in our brains,
like the instinct of a snagged fish drowning,
diving for the bottom,
where the deep mud darkness breathes
and waits to take us back.

FIRE IN STEUBENVILLE

Each time I come back home
something else has burned.
The abandoned Pennsylvania station—
where years ago I stood in fog
and listened for the train
to Washington, D.C.,
and later, in the sooty afternoons,
laid pennies on the rails
for mainline freights
to flatten thin as knife-blades—
that station was the first to go.
Black smoke charred a hundred
slag-gray pigeons;
scorched rats ran downtown
toward the river.
Across the street, in Pug's Hotel,
a dozen winos rubbed their eyes,
and chucked their old timetables.

Then, Pug's Hotel itself,
where a group of Harvard scholars,
come to study smoke and smoke's effects
upon the city stayed.
Their files and Cambridge pinstripes
make good kindling.

Then, a warehouse
down on Fifth Street.
Ten football fields of carpets

unrolled into flame,
and up and down the street,
firemen hosed the smoking homes of
out-of-town Italians.

Then, a lumberyard,
a pharmacy, a bingo hall.
The sidewalks buckled,
women wandered
in the alleys
toward the Holy Name Cathedral.

No arrests were made.
In Steubenville,
fire—in one form or another,
whether open hearth, arc-welder,
or the bitter smolder of old mines—
pays its million-dollar bribes.
Fire, that bright-faced hit man of good steel,
that roaring goon of coal,
has bought off all the cops,
and keeps the mayor
gagged and sweating
in his office.
In the meantime,
my city that has fed on fire so long
is now itself fire's feeding.

At night, downtown,
I clamber over cinders and split boards,

calling names against the darkness,
listening for echoes
from walls no longer there.
Ash swirls overhead like bats.
In a hundred smoky South End rooms,
Polish women
start awake
to mill-screams, sirens,
the cries of fire-haired girls,
and men lob dynamite
into their own homes
from the streets.

WHAT KATY DID

Another effect . . . was for long the appallingly high rate of insanity
of farmers' wives, whether on the frontier or on isolated farms. . . .
"Loneliness," *Dictionary of American History,* Vol. 3

At the base of the wings is the organ with which the male katydid
argues whether "Katy did" or "Katy didn't." Katy, unlike most female
insects, can faintly make her own sounds but she apparently rarely
does so unless much disturbed. —Frank E. Lutz, *Fieldbook of Insects.*

It's an old song
(so we tell the children)
sung a thousand times a day
by heat's harmless
leaf-like cricket,
the green that ticks
in gardens north and south,
that sometimes rides
a child's hair
toward the house
or freezes, disappearing,
in the weeds.
It's a kind of folksong,
so we say.

Well,
what Katy did,
I'll tell you:

rode a wagon
all the way from Pennsylvania
to Ohio,
ruined kidneys,
weakened spleen,
dropped a dead child
near a Chillicothe saltlick;

chopped brush and tallgrass
near the Shawnee town
two summers for her kitchen patch
while the old man wandered drunk
on headbust near the river;

lost three toes
one winter, cut them off herself
to stave gangrene,
then an hour later
nursed her newborn child;

ate squirrel and possum and pigeon
half-cooked on her thinwood fire,
never touched a drop of liquor;

then, four years at that place,
grown thin and crazy in the leanness of her days,
killed, one howling night, her daughters
with a skillet
when she dreamed a bear
dressed like an Indian
had raped them;

9

killed her husband
come home from six weeks'
hunting in Kentucky;

killed the hound,
killed the measly chickens,
burned the cabin,
pulled the corn
and let it lay,
then set out,
never stopping,
never eating,
five days down the river,

swam across a creek one night
and hanged herself
from a willow by a rock.

Is what Katy did,
did Katy.

Will you tell this,
katydid,
will you tell this
to the children?

IN THE WOODS BEYOND THE COAL FIELDS

I have come here to forget
the red god of my fathers
and the furnace of his meaning.
But the breeze is westerly today,
hauls Ohio's sin here.
Far across these Seven Ranges
float smoke and coalspill,
which to this summer's common wounds
upon the hillside, field,
and pond
apply no healing poultice.
The large, warm woman of the air
who once nursed blighted fox
and split-branched tree,
who once spilled health like splashed weeds
up and down these hollows,
hobbles now, hammered
in the darkness of old mines.
I will not find her here,
but I cannot go away.

In a dream that stalks me like my doom,
I fall through all the daylight
of these woods,
and stumble upstream toward the mine,
where the rotting bodies
of my fathers
slip like nightmares
from black slag.

WATCHING BISON AT THE STATE PRESERVE, NOBLE COUNTY, OHIO

Above the crest of Injun Ridge the sky
planed southward, scarred with clouds,
November twilight making raw gold
of the distant buckskin ridges.
Hep and Brud and I scuffed bootsoles
in the slate and smoked.
Below us, ConCoal's newest canyon,
strewn with limestone, shale, and shattered trees,
gathered yellow water in its gullet.
"That's coal juice, poison," Hep said.
He flicked his smoke and smoothed
the black scope from its sheath,
watched a far hawk glide
then settle. Then he settled,
the scope stone-still, stone-cold
in his steady hand.

Beyond the mine pit, the state fence
hung high and gray
against the slipping hillside.
"To keep them from that water,"
Hep said. "There's a fresh pond
down the far side of the ridge.
That's where they wallow in the summer.
This here's the closest you can get
to see them."

Brud stamped his feet and blew breath out
in a cold cloud. I looked, and saw them,

down the tumbling, undercut hill.
Dusky as the brushfired oaks and maples
they lay beneath,
they watched weather
scramble over unfamiliar landscape
in the distance:
cloud over rock, scud over weedshock,
cold over galled goldenrod.

They did not move.
Nowhere to go.
This cold and small Ohio.

And as we turned to leave,
to skid down coal-dust roads
toward evening in the hollows,
toward Hep's bitter whiskey, Brud's cold stove,
my own wind-drilled, temporary home,
crows cawed from the pit,
and everywhere, a sour wind was rising.

HORSE CARCASS

Even the meanest painters
of America
have no brushes for this,
but slouch from their canvas sick and ashamed.
No mother would dream it
even on her deathbed in the asylum.

But two men are allotted the job,
disposers of auto-wrecked bull,
skunk-smutch stinking on shoulders, dog-hide dried to the road.

Beauticians of the highways!
Even the hairs of their heads
are combed toward the county seat!
Their overalls like winding sheets,
with spades and trowels
they hew and peel the flesh off
down to clean.
All day they do it.
All day they curse the stupidity of beasts.

But soon it is night.
A dark stain makes the shape of horse
on the road to Steubenville.
The men lunge and buck in their dreams,
mounting the ghosts of their lives.
Bones snap. Hearts burst
a furlong from home.

Huge bruises spread like the snowfall,
under whose cold they crawl like dark snakes,
dodging the hooves of white horses.

WINTER SNAKES

All week I've watched
this sod buck with frost,
this hollow's crumbling edge
where spring flood
washes down
drowned woodchucks
every year.
Freeze heaves
the pried, black soil:
it breaks and
spills
and hits the hollow ice
below like buckshot.
I clamber down
the steep hardrock
so deep into this place
I lose the sun.
Cold climbs and hangs
around my hips.

Land's guts, coils
of clay, the untouched rib
of slate, the
root-claw clutching
stone and ice
are still. No deep hearts
pulse here in December.
But I lift a trap of rock,
disclosing darkness,

darkness,
and they lie there, by the hundreds,
a thick blacklash of serpent,
cold and brittle as the air
that cracks around them.
Light clubs the frozen ground.
Sumacs lean and tick
in wind.

An old and lost existence,
as if rising from an ancient stump or barrow,
uncoils inside me,
dull, cold, blunt-headed:
the month's bleak urge
unclamps me, joint by joint,
till their long coats fit me like my skin.

SNAG

When I slept in the creek,
it was winter. Not a rock talked,
not a star turned.
I was alone with water,
watched and watching,
as I slept the long freeze out.
In the spring I turned
in my hammock of sand,
slung between shores
like a net,
and dipped my dark leg
to the bedrock,
stood fast against the flood.
In summer now, I rise
high above the water,
collecting land-wrack and foam,
steering the creek to my left and my right,
arranging the shape
of this farm,
filling a slough,
making my place by degrees.

At night I cast terrible shadows.
The ghosts of the drowned,
like birds clinging close to the trunk,
sneak silently down my black branches.

WOMEN ON PORCHES OUTSIDE HANNIBAL, OHIO

All are women I lack the strength
to love or live with.
They walk easy in the starlight
of poor counties
where the richest men around
pack their cellars
with potatoes,
sell postcards,
marry girls
to farm boys who have death
inside them
like the engine
in a car,
or, gone all crazy
with the sun,
shout Isaiah
at the buzzards in their fields.

Already, I digress.
I cannot keep these women long in focus.
They keep drifting off,
slow clouds
at the edge of darkness,
full of rain.
And whatever field my body is
lies fallow
as great thistles
thicken on all sides,
blocking light.

Soon I cannot see at all.
Even the clouds are somewhere else.
What have I done,
what have I never known to do?

I turn myself restlessly over
and over,
raising bleary dustcrops
in a childless drought,
all
seed.

NIGHTWATCH

Between the woman and her flesh
exists a darkness
in which secret constellations
constantly align
and realign
according to her
shifting pole
of strife.
Sometimes the high bright star
is birth, and wheeling
all around it
are the beasts of breach
mid-pain,
their eyes the greatest minor stars.
All have moving lights
within the coalsacks of their bellies,
slowly migratory,
pulsing,
     dimming,
          pulsing.

Man sees them through
her skin
in darker nights,
so cannot sleep,
nor can he ever
slide so softly
into her
that something of him knows
her unknown place.

He lies awake,
watching as a five-starred
seabird, lynx, or dragon
glimmers forth,
revolves around the axis
of her spine, and
casts its pale blue
light between
them on the sheets—
that shallow, fading river
none of his kind
can ever cross.

LAST OF AUGUST RIVER POEM

It is evening: last light
white as bridal clothes
falls upon this broad Ohio's shoaling.
Minnows nibble at the surface of the air,
and the upshore dreaming
of a lone man fishing
drifts past me like
his uncaught, secret carp.

Above Kentucky, the moon
is one wheel turning
on the black road of the night.
A young man wanders
in the locust trees
across the river.
He is looking for the girl
he sees each time he sleeps.

The river moves its freight
of fish and silt and darkness
past him deeper
than it ever has.
He will not sleep
until it ceases,
or his girl
slips up
from the river
to leave her footprints
gleaming on the stones.

As for myself,
I do not pity him or envy him.
I have long forgotten
all the girls I swam toward
in the dark.

I lean back in the willows
saying nothing,
needing nothing,
waiting for the great blue heron,
down from lonely Ghent or Milton,
bringing dawn.

At the End of a Love Affair

1

In the woods, the closer quiet centers
in a beech stump
and takes shape.
Far off, the bluejays racket
in the pines.
Every stone in the creek
is closing its mouth,
the coal dust sparkles
on a snag,
the bones of a dog
jut from the washed-out bank.
Old shoes. Glass.
The poisonous smoke
of the puffballs.

2

Waking up, the afternoon ·
cicada grinds loudly in the hickory.
The faint bells of the Dutchman's-breeches
move from east to west,
east to west,
with the breeze.
As I turn my head,
a chipmunk whistles,
leaping toward the lesser panic
of the weeds.

I'd give all I have
to meet it in that trembling dark
and talk,
to crawl inside its little
world of husks and stems
and settle toward
that easy peace
of beasts.

3
But when I stand, I know
again: I am not all
invisible.
Everywhere there is a drawing in,
a tautening.

Only the delicate leaves
of the poplar
keep turning, turning, turning
aimlessly and do not see
or smell me.
Body, I am sinking slowly
toward the sadness
of my country,
toward the slow but urgent
earth
of wilderness I've fled to:
patience, flesh,
and silence.

What she humanly,
in madness, love, and suffering
could not,
this quiet wood
might tell us.

But we must die
our cursed, keen-sensed
though bachelor death,
to know.

OCTOBER

He has heaved his last hay
under roof. The cedar waxwings
disappear, one by one,
all day.
The hill road kills another drunk,
come sundown:
the wrecked car darkens
in the dust,
fills with flies.
A fox barks
in the dark field
where he spent his sweat
for hours.

He takes his whiskey
to the hilltop, where
night is never accomplished.
He can make out cows
like rocks along a windbreak
far below.
The creek runs through
its willowed tunnel
like a small girl
talking in her sleep.

Soon, the curse or spell is on him.
He lies, face down,
in a fume of whiskey,
arms thrown out,

his flesh like
fresh snow on old bones,
a century of cold.

In his yearly habit
he sleeps deep
where sometime in the night
the big wind
comes against the county
and his rich fields
fail, again,
toward winter.

THE BODY OF A MAN WASHED UP

1

His hands are thin-skinned
as amoebae.
You can see clear through
to blue bone and the veins
as small as needles.
With those hands
he built his house upon the land,
and it stood strong
against the weather.

Now, his arms are pins of wood,
brittle lengths of cane,
and his chest an old cast flat-iron
left to rust
along some hidden creek-bed
where his wife
has never been.
His sex
is knobby ginseng,
two small galls
in moss.

2

The heron's eye regards
you from a willow,
blinks once, a nugget
quickly tarnished,
and goes out.

Far out on the water
a small bird skims that
silver,
darts away.
A crawfish clambers
on an oily rock.

The sun sets,
the river stills,
and from his snag-
gashed throat
silt spills,
making death's
last word,

a kind of little shore.

SOWBUGS

No one hears your snortings
in the loam and gloom
behind Hub Baker's shed.
Few go so close aground
as you do, few people
that I know.
But drunk one Sunday night,
a friend of mine fell down,
spun groundward
to the leaves and mud
among the humid precincts
of your homeland.
A Brobdingnag of fume,
he opened eye
to stay his swirling,
spied your rooting
in a mess of fallen weeds,
and forgot his state and place,
grew small.
He saw you and your brothers
barge blind against each other in
your hurries,
saw you all roll up
like chevroned pills,
then, as minutes passed,
unroll again,
and launch yourselves
like triremes, fifty-oared,
across the rough seas
of the garden.

He smelled your eatings,
spent beetles,
snail eggs,
rotting straw
and soot.
Alone in all the empty loudness
of his world,
he fell to yours,
and found a busy home
forgotten since young Adam
spoke your tongue.

Later, sobered up,
he came to me
and tried to tell it.
We sat together on the porch,
beetles mumbling riddles
on the floor,
moths pronouncing
pleasure at the light.

We drank to you,
drank to all that lives unheeded,
and listened, wordless,
hours into night.

WHERE I COME FROM
THERE ARE WOMEN WEEPING

In their narrow houses
they are sleeping
on clean sheets.
Outside, the river
turns and spreads,
and folds itself
upon the shore
like batch on batch of laundry.
It will never come all clean.

Now their husbands
clamber from the mines
to drink between
the shadows
of the bridge.

One rolls a cigarette
with flecked, arthritic hands.
He is nearly dead
with weather.
Heat is in him
like a broken glass.

No flood this year,
though sluggish carp,
like sandbags,
heap against the shore.

Who will walk across
those mud-dull backs
toward God and Weirton, West Virginia?

Not the mayor.
Not these men.
Not the ghost of Edwin Stanton.

No one.

An Unsent Letter of Darwin's

When it closes down,
this world of forms, and it will,
you will be strolling along some beach in Virginia,
in America.
You will be alone: the season will be summer.
Far upwind from you
your father will slouch
under an endlessly falling darkness,
and lie down down in the dunes
on his bed of sand.

There will be porpoises dying beyond the surf:
whales will roll their dun, sunken bellies
moonward,
and many ancient sailors will shipwreck there and be lost.

In the city, the scientists
will shrink from their suits and be gone,
the dusts of mathematics.
All the great clocks will stop,
their tenders fallen headlong in the gears,
lunch pails left open on the scaffolds.

The churches will fill
with dead souls, rising up walls
like salt water.
There will be insects in the
alms box,
dying in their paper nests.

And you will be strolling along some beach in Virginia,
alone, in the summer,
like a lemur's your hands growing small-boned and thin,
your eyes larger and larger,
watching the terrible waves slowly cease,
stop soothing themselves,
so good-bye

COMING OUT OF ICE

Thoreau in the final pages of *Walden* creates a myth about a despised
worm that surmounts death and bursts from its hidden chamber in a
wooden table. Was the writer dreaming of man, man freed at last
from the manacles of ice? —Loren Eiseley

I try to think of things that might
be slower: the voyaging, footless sperm
that flails upstream
inside a standing woman,
heat leaking from a huge gold stone
in the center of a field,
a dead man waking bit by bit
amid the constellations of the sea. . .

The cheetahs of the seasons
fell their breathless prey.
Lightning lashes in the treetops.
Water races everywhere,
smacking its silver lips.

But I am outside speed:
I have lived so long, so slow,
I saw the place where darkness
splashed forth light,
where fire bit off its finger
and made man.
In all that time, I've
taken breath but once.

My heart's dilation
outlasts the fish-thick, blinding sea's.

My destination
is a new green season, whose
rumors have come down
amid the glacier's
bouldered groan and grind.
It seems as distant as a god,
but I have patience,
and my eyes see everywhere.

I am coming out of ice, slowly
out of ice, breaking frost's locks,
breaking the zero chains.

When I breathe again
even the color of air will change:
men will shadow their tongues
with fresh sounds
and hot-blooded beasts
will breed toward new kinds
in a sunlight the shape of my world.

II ❧ LISTENING TO THE VOICES

When no sign manifests itself, it is
provoked. For example, a sort of
evocation is performed with the
help of animals; it is they who
show what place is fit to receive
the sanctuary or the village.

—Mircea Eliade,
The Sacred And The Profane

HOUNDS

What howl down hollows
in this county in the night
will heel or sit all day
for feed or rags to sleep on.
But come the dark, they need
nothing of the hand that picked
the ticks from ears or crowns
or rubbed their muzzles roughly.
No—down the hollows howling,
doubled, tripled, packed on hunt,
they run the fox or deer
more deeply into coves and gullies
than they ever can come back from.
But they do. In the morning, one by one,
they amble up the hillsides
trailing briars from their tails,
slack-tongued, panting,
their keen teeth sheathed again
in the forenoon fullness
that their drowsy patience knows
will spill another meat-rich midnight
on the hills before them, for their hunger.

NIGHT

Out Broomstick,
kids dig ginseng
from the white oak shade,
then go home, sacks
and pockets swollen
with rich healing.
Long after they have gone,
a great oak, girdled by
a fall of rock
last winter,
lets loose its dense upholding
heft from hillside,
plunges,
and upon a boulder
full of fossils splits.

At home, the kids are dreaming wildly
and their bed bucks
white oak planks
so loud their father rises.

In the dark
he hears their footsteps
on the floor.

Don't fall, he thinks,
don't fall.

SPARROWS DRINKING

The harmony of the universe is alternately tensed and relaxed, like a lyre or bow. —*Symposium*

Clouds float, lax amoebae in the ditch.
Breeze throws bright seines
on the water, catching only glints.

Down from poplar crowns
and oakspars drift the sparrows,
loose as seed or thistledown.

Tentative, they gather at the edge,
dipping quick bills as if stitching
water to the ditch's verge.

Then they burst away. They swerve,
unknotting into flight,
over raveled bindweed toward loosestrife
and seamless sprawls of spurge.

SOMETIMES I AM LOOKING

Sometimes I am looking
for the rusty feather
of the vulture
near the path's edge
where it settled, dim and dry,
abandoned
in the downdraft of a dream.
Sometimes I am looking
for the snakeskin
crackling in the hickory branch,
where black-backed beetles
cut it scale by scale apart
into a kind of food,
transparent, weightless as an eye.
Sometimes I am looking
for the deer's fresh
birthing place,
the thin grass blue-red,
rising,
steaming still.
And sometimes I am looking
for the clearing
where a huge oak
wrestles up from
massive roots
to shade
a banked and mossy shed
in which
a man I never knew

cried once
into the darkness,
pulled the sheet
up to his chin,
and left, to tremble
always in the
halt arms of the leaves
and cobs and
husks,
that sound,
this sound,

our own.

LISTENING FOR GOD

Drifting in and out of sleep
beside the river,
I dream that I expect him.
My body cleans itself
of the poison of the night.
It is like the river,
moving mindlessly
toward health.
My head steadies,
light grows clearer.

On the sand beneath the willows,
near my tent, my dog
lies peacefully awake.
She is neat
with the neatness of animals,
wasting nothing,
hoarding nothing.
Morning is a perfect comfort
she can breathe in
as easily as air.
Her life seems better than a man's,
for she is speechless,
she suffers nothing
like the whirling madness
men name language.

Because of her purer kind of silence,
I think she hears him
long before I do.

Yesterday, he might have been
faint birdsong,
far down on the river,
and the day before,
the dim roar
of the jet stream,
ten miles up.

But here, this morning,
near these sloughs of rising light,
I know that I will have him,
know that I will hear him
speak my clearly human tongue.

Suddenly,
behind me in the trees,
clinging to a plunging willow branch,
so green I cannot see him,
he clicks and hums,
this time a katydid,
to warn me.

MOTHS ABOVE THE FIRE

All good men's daughters who have died
must return like this,
intent, colored like leaves,
above their fathers' fires.
Though drawn, they do not
touch the flames;
night grows richer
all around them
so that space, that widow
who reminds men
of their losses,
silently retires.

Times like these
are the Easters of the heart.

Sitting with men
around fires,
I think of trilliums
in the deep Ohio woods
whose petals are tongues
that speak to drowned mice
and to broken fireflies,
saying
arise, arise.

ONE FOR ANNIE

I was in the mountains
when you came to me.
You were humming,
humming.
I was in the far woods
where I'd found a carved rock
by Cook's Creek,
and you came to me,
like a single, slim-winged insect,
and you sang what light means
gently, at my ear.
Tonight, I walked down Brown's Run
to the old house
where wrecked beds
lie rusting in the weeds.
I sat down on a flathead stump,
but I longed to
turn in somewhere,
you beside me,
and to lay my hand
to root there
in your hair.
Annie, I longed to
have you, as I never can,
all around me always,
like the air.

WHAT TO WATCH FOR IN THE COUNTRY

The sand-like rust
on a hinge,
shirtsleeves,
the silver
of turned soil,
its soft hunks slowly
drying down
to brown.

Hemp rope,
leather,
barn beams.

The milksnake
in the hay.
The fieldmouse
rambling through
the briar.

Rock-dust teeth
of catfish, and the
thick hide of
the creek-rock,
and the pale skin
of the schoolteacher,
alone in her dusty cabin,
plunging her hands
in cold water.

STORM

Outside, a blacksnake raids the wren-box.
High pipings shrill downridge
like fever, then are gone
much sooner than seems decent.

No.

Far off, above dark Hartshorn Ridge,
thunderheads are building,
and I must let the lightning judge or not
that oak snag on its bald
where foxes
sleep among old bones.

TIES

In this first effective sun
the creosote is loosed
and beads in oily glimmers
on the ties.
It raises hell's high smell
above the dead, left weeds.
Forever wood, held back
from bleeding into soil,
split lengthwise,
plated and spiked with iron,
the ties stay longer whole
than hefty men.

Abandoned by the
right-of-way in heaps,
they keep snow cold
weeks longer
than rock piles, stacks of tile,
the trash of creeks.

But come summer,
match them and they burn for days.
The smoke they make
kills cancer, flies, and rats.

I have never known
a tie
to burn completely down.

I think their ashes
must be magic—

I rub them on
my face and arms,

to last.

GARDENING

I listen as the wrens again hurl music
from the sumacs by the garden. Discing done,
my neighbor drives the creek road, having paid
his kind attention to my land. I labor
in the flood of noon to mark the rows.
I dream of healthy greenness that will come.

Sometimes I hear this land ask, "Have you come
for my health, or for yours?" Each year, I labor
all the winter, till the blizzard's done,
to know my answer. Then the peeper's music
rustles mind's old reeds: I think of rows
green again. All attention paid

Seems for nothing. Yet it was better paid
to hearing that old question than to come
to some conclusion. What's answered may be done.
But this is work unfinished, this ongoing music
of man's old tune, played upon the rows—
this rich chord struck in spring's endless labor.

Now, the bees above the garden labor
hiveward, heavy with the pollen come
from blossoming persimmons. Their visits paid
all morning to the honeysuckle rows
and clovers, they gather all that's daily done
to ripeness in their gold combs full of music.

I too am a denizen who hears the music
rising from the dailiness of labor.
To this green place in the mountains I have come,
healthy as a sapling, hoping my rows
will richen like those hives. What I've paid
in sweat and thirst and work is what I've done

To keep me from a life that ends not done,
but eagerly unfinished. May what will come
lift me from the misbegotton labor
of my times, from the shrill inhuman music
of the city, from health's wages never paid.
May I gain the strength of planted rows:

May the months grow sweeter, like honey come
from hives of bees when daily labor's done.
Health's paid: let music fill these rows.

III ❧ THE PLACE WHERE YOU STAND

Put off thy shoes from thy feet,
for the place where thou standest
is holy ground.

—Exodus

COCOON

All winter I have watched
it from my window,
gray bundle at the branch-tip
like a bandage.
Nuthatch and chickadee
have picked its weathered husk;
a few strands dangle
from its weft.

Now spring winds
harp through slender branches,
pluck the lyres
of bowed forsythias
across the soggy garden.

Not long from now,
some night aswirl
with riverings of scent
will rise up from the ground,
as I will rise up,
strangely called,
from bed.

Barefoot in the misty dark,
I will stand beneath
that branch
to see the gauze split back
and part,

to see the season's first great healing
fruit brilliantly alive,
pause to dry its wings,
then drift off
down the ripening air
toward the ecstasies of heat,
joy's summer nourishments,
riches dear as blood.

STANDING STILL

I have come a long way just to do this;
I am old, and it is hard as being born.
All around me in this woods the leaves are
moving in the breeze—flashing,
turning, falling—there are insects rising
and descending in the shadows and the light,
stones are rolling in the running water
of the creek.

Once, I wished to climb the inward darkness
of big trees, labor upward to the leaves, and launch
myself like fog off blowing branches.
Once, I wanted plunging like the bass,
and dreamed of green stones tumbling near my belly
like cold eggs.

Now, my mother's body calls to me from the stillness.
From the crest of Dye's Ridge
large birds can rest their wings
upon a downward stream of air and,
without moving them, soar between big trees
into shadows rich with all I do not know.

So enough of quickness and of noise, enough
of strength and fury, and the dance of death
they measure. Now I know my mother's age,
I know the meaning of her years.
I linger here beside the standing water of this ditch
and speak to her across it, through the mist.

The water does not tremble with our voices.
Nothing moves away from us into the twilight.
Everything is still.

Let me learn this stillness deeply in the night,
let it live inside me without ceasing,
let it fill me with its power and its substance.
Let me wake as wise as stone or wood
when upon this dark, unmoving hill
bursts tomorrow's faithful light.

NIGHT STOP AT THE CROSSROADS

Where we started from
that time, city's high summer
bred its thick prose
choked with detail,
so we drank our way
across the state
till dark fell
like a single, simple line.

In the Crossroads Bar
at Malaga, Ohio,
we took the table
closest to the night
that poured fragrant
through the door,
and shot pool
until the bright felt
bleared, until
the gaudy balls
in dawn's light
softened.

Then, down 26 from Rich Fork
clear to Graysville,
laughing, weary,
we recalled our
better shots,
and dreamed of shots
we'd take.

And for a time,
we were satisfied
that our lives, our worlds,
were as certain as our games,
and that the fog,
as it did that time,
would roll
forever cool across
the creek and road,
forever true and steady
toward familiar corners.

MARY DAUGHERTY

When she stands like this
in rain beside the road,
I remember all the iron
she's taken from
her father.
When the oil pipe broke his back,
a man from Antioch, Ohio
waved snakes above his bed
and Mary watched, believing.

From her mother, Mary has
the strength of clay,
and the power that is given
certain women by their gardens,
by their summers,
by their birthings and their mendings.

From her brothers, Mary has
the joy of talking back,
and the honor of
many fistfights, won and lost.

From her sisters, Mary has
the promise of early childbirth,
and a taste for
wildness:
berry,
beechnut,
and the rare
mayapple.

WILD TURKEY, STATE ROUTE 280

Nearly unexpected as a dinosaur,
that heron-high, steady-gaited hen
crossing, in high sunshine,
the clay dust of the logging road.
Twenty years ago, one fogbound
Greenbrier morning, I heard the last one
an hour before sunup,
and leaped from my bunk for gladness.

Then the long silence commenced.
Through two hermit's summers
in my twenties,
I sneaked over the hill,
lurking in lightless sumacs,
listening for the downridge tom.
Only the creek warbled,
distant in the darkness.

Today, I lay the worry down
that I carried those two decades:
the bird is back,
grown fat on beech and hazelnut.
At the farm some summer morning, slipping
from a dream,
I will wake to its call in the hollow,
and roll at last contentedly back to sleep,
warm with a relic of wildness
here, alive, recovered.

CURES

Some old men I know
eat weeds that blossom
in their dooryards.
Others gnash down bits of coal
as if to set themselves afire.
Coltsfoot, ginseng,
even kerosene, tall tales:
from anything, the people of this county
invent their special cures
to heal themselves,
their children, and their stock,
and day and night,
health burns brightly
on each ridge.

Inside a shack
a mile down Wolf Pen Hollow,
a woman makes her kind of cure
upon a mandolin,
which has, in turn,
been made of one good gourd.
She says the strings
are bobcat gut,
the keys old musket barrels
heated, hammered, drilled, and shaped.
She says that music makes her laugh,
and laughter cures old age.

In the light of stars
I often sleep beneath,
having overcome the weakness
of the roof,
the pain of doors that close,
the plagues of proof and fact,
doubt is a disease,
and all the healthy lies
I've come to learn
are cures,
cures as powerful as lightning,
whose bolts hit trees
I know exist,
and can hike to in the morning
to touch hot heartwood
trued to dream's hard temper.

GREENBRIER PORTRAITS

UNCLE BUCKLEY

On a porch in Ozark, Ohio
this man with water in his face:
clear eyes twin springs
beneath gray up-country hickories,
wet hollows in the dark of white oak slopes;
nose a flood-scoured prow of sandstone
outcropped from a creek bank's south exposure;
forehead broad, a furrowed
bald once wild with sumac thatch;
two downridge gullies running
to the corners of his mouth.

Under his smile
white stones gleam,
lucky quartzes
smooth as an Angus's grinders,
sweet with talk of greenness,
good to whistle through.

OLD MAN MACKEY

Hat Mackey's skin
the color of old horseshoes,
rust of brakedrums, universals
off old Fords. Arms
lean as axles, he lifts
the young pig
from the worm-fenced pen,

sets it down,
claps the thick dust
from his palms,
muscles rippling, working—

cords of hardwood by the chimney,
fenceposts weathered forty years.

MRS. BUELL, SUNDAY
In her holy ghost smock
and bishopy hair,
she fishes by the Clear Fork,
singing, "To Sleep by Thee Oh Jesus."
In her shoes
the color of heavenly palominos,
she fishes by the Clear Fork,
singinging, "The Lord Is My Rest and My Peace."
In her hat
like a clutch of white doves,
she fishes by the Clear Fork,
singing, "Safe in the Ark of Our Savior."

In her dark-fingered gloves
made of serpents,
in her shawl
like a fire made of vestments,
through her teeth that are older than Calvin,
she sings, "Nearer My God to Thee,"
and her Lord flashes bright,
like a bluegill at bait,
in the wild, pentecostal waters.

DRUNK JIMMY WETZEL'S WITTY

A boy as small as a grackle.
Rides like Jesus on the dashboard.
Eyes flash red and green.
Hair like moss-whorls on an acorn.
Eyes flash red and green.
Talks back to the sheriff.
Tells lies to deaf old women.
Chews hickory sticks and needles.
Eyes flash red and green.

The pet of every pretty girl.
Sips whiskey from a thimble.
Eyes flash red and green, O
Eyes flash red and green.

BOY FISHING

Wild hair orange as broomsage
ripe in autumn, forehead
smeared with chrisms—pond mud,
slick juice off a catfish—
knees resurrecting through
his jeans
like fingers knuckled through
a dusty glove,
feet butt-tucked,
spine readied in its perfect curve,
he sits hunching
in the warm day's womb,
umbilicaled to greenness
rank with jumping things.

In the sudden tautness
of his line,
in a heave of
August waters,
comes each hour
his deliverance.

COUNTRY MATTERS

In June, the older sisters,
many named for flowers—
Viburnum, Trillium, Aster—
sit by the Clear Fork
with their clothes off,
languid, lounging,
braiding their bright hair.
They eat berries,
or the first soft peaches
from the farm.
Later, when they stand and stretch,
when they smooth the stems and weedbits
from their buttocks and their thighs
then wade into the water,
small shoals of bluegills flash
between their knees,
and nip the fine hairs there.

Each night, across the county,
the older sisters lean together
in their perfumed upstairs windows,
away from the coarse and keen-eared brothers,
speaking secret things in secret voices,
voices trembling
like warm water
riffling over stones.

MORNING, LATE SUMMER

I wake up in the morning, in the quiet country.
The birds transform themselves
from tree to tree, an aerial foliage of singing
out of dreams.
Even water beating on the sheet of tin
beside the smokehouse is a magic,
an echo of the heartbeats
of the beasts in far-off fields.

By my window, a phoebe nests.
Her mate comes ten times an hour,
every hour of the day.
They do not change,
while all around them everything is changed,
toward endings
thick with smoke and harvests.

Down the road, a neighbor works his pump,
its rusty shriek a shitepoke
in a swamp,
fog rolling in,
some damp November noon.

SUMMER SOLSTICE

At noontime, listless, sweating on the porch,
I heard my neighbor's daughters
ride their ponies
through the grove of apple trees.
Beyond them, where they rode toward,
the thicket in their wild south acres,
I knew a blacksnake
in a sweetgum
fattened on wren chicks,
and a redbud, blooming far too late,
rashed with too-rich sweetness
all the thick air
they would ride through.

In my mind, I followed them.
And then I went no further.
I let those daughters ride beyond me,
to the steaming bottoms half a mile past Wolf Pen,
to the warm, mossed rocks of Sunfish,
to the rank horsetails of Cranesnest.
For I know these sweating days
will shorten now:
in the shrinking summer light
those girls will turn their ponies
each day sooner homeward.
Come October,
I will step out glad to greet them.
In the clear, cool air,
they will be smiling;

their seasoned faces will be wiser,
more gently flushed than now,
like persimmons ripened by first frost.

OTHERS

1

Touching you tonight, I hear
their names through all the voices
of your body, now spoken gently
from your breasts,
now firmly
from your thighs.
I do not know
what answer
I can give them.

2

Late in the evenings, by the river,
in the shadows of the levee cottonwoods,
this world your body
was many times a place
I no longer lived in,
an excited Egypt
far from all the common counties
of Ohio
I am made of.
Strange birds fluttered in your valleys,
singing secret languages
like hieroglyphics.

3

Now you lie beside me
in this twilight room.
The faint light from the window
sweeps across your body

I am not alone.
I am merely one of many
in a world I did not seek,
a new world rich with others' names.
I must learn them,
learn them all,
to know you once again.
I must speak them
in my plain tongue,
in my plain way,
to understand.

But when you wake,
when you turn to me again,
when you touch my arm,
my face, my side,
will I know those names
your fingertips will speak?

Will I know
what answer I can give them?
Will I speak the language
you so sweetly,
but so distantly
have learned?

OTHERS: HER REPLY

Touching you tonight, I hear
within me speaking
all of those I've loved:
the dark ones
I pressed my thighs to
in the shadows by the river,
the pale ones,
seeking poems in the trembling
that they brought me,
the bright ones,
making worlds and names
of the simple, naked laughter
that we shared.

I have found myself,
and I am full of them.
I hear their names
in rain, in rivers,
and in you.
They have made us richer.

When I touch you,
when I love you
through the years,
you will hear them
whisper,
Brother, brother,
we have blessed you.

SENSE
  for Jim Winland

1

Coppery the smell of radish
wafered red-edged on the steel
of his old case knife.
Retired, back-countried,
simplified to one room
stocked with dust, sunlight,
and tobacco,
near penniless
save for small change
and these red-skinned roots
he eats,
O he eats, eats
and smiles after,
his thought's creel crammed
with rock bass, smallmouth,
sweet sunfish.

2

Fools will go the long way
to the fishing spot
by the road, in trucks ungainly
as mammoths in bogs, mired
in rock-flour and clay washouts,
sucked down
axle-deep in the hillside's
damp migration.

Hurry gets them nowhere,
dizzy in the dead-end sunlight
of some gully,
while above them, everywhere,
landscape—weed, rock,
fencepost—
adventures slowly
toward its far, eventual seasons.

But a man
"with three cents' worth of sense"
will walk the creek itself,
gladly leave the road
for the eternity
of the stream's green afternoon,
feet learning wisdom and balance and grace
from stones,
eyes keen
for the dark overbites of roots
where the long, under-sycamore bass
lie tasting the water's bringing.

3
Such steady coming and going,
sure-footed, based in the world,
always half-hungry though
grinning,
is the fuel whose fire is good sense,
the blazing round his heart,
spreading bright through the wealth of his veins,

smelting hot the habitat of joy—
his intricate, sensible body.

4

So, for strength, for lasting,
count this man's regular laughter,
loud in the afternoon—
the strong bass striking,
his own clownish lunge from a stone,
the kingfisher diving
will start it.
For sense,
tally his days,
his stringer of rockbass flashing in sun
or his sunfish still shining
past midnight
in the warm rills of moon
as he rests on his porch,
thumbing three pennies,
the richest man in this county.

MOOSE RIDGE APPLE WINE

1

In August, on the township roads,
the blacksnakes stretch themselves
across the rocks and hard clays
so you have to stop the car.
Then they coil themselves,
lift their slim, sleek heads,
and twitch their tails like rattlers.
If you grab them,
you will find how hot the world is
in the summer,
and your hands will smell like dead meat
for three days.

2

In the roadside ditches
where the weeds twist thick,
the minor lizards—skinks and swifts—
tour the sticks and tendrils
with quick eyes. Beetles glint
like jewelry on the undersides of leaves,
deerflies choir on mouse skulls,
green cutworms slash at thin stems
with their sharp and sidewise jaws.
On a smooth stick, invisible as air,
a mantis hacks a small wasp into splinters,
holds a flash of wing in claw.

3

Sober, high-noon seeing,
these sudden sightings from the car:
these stumps, these cold springs splashing on the rocks,
these dead hawks in the mulleins,
with the black and yellow beetles
big as nickels on their wings.
Things to see, to make a lifetime of,
to carry home or drowse on,
to curl a dream around.

4

But daylight lasts a long time
in the summer: it is not yet time for sleeping.
And now, the old Ford hot from climbing,
the big woods break
along a saddleback of ridge,
sunlight shimmers on a gatepost,
and in the middle of a field
of thistles, joe-pye-weed, and nettles
sits Mr. Hummel's shack.
A thousand silver dollars
in the mortar of the mantel,
and a cask of double eagles under floorboards!
And Mr. Hummel, confident, at ease,
sits smiling on the porch
as you pull in on the gravel.
When you unfold, sweating, from the car,
katydids whirr off in all directions,
and a house wren rides the high scale
in the buckeye by the porch.

Moose Ridge, August,
Hummel's apple wine!

5

Around here, men who have the time,
and men who make the time,
sit all day at Hummel's,
and they let their extra money leak away
like rain down Wolf Pen Creek,
then heal their empty places
with Hummel's home-made wine.
His moon-eyed hound that rocks
and hobbles on its three good legs
won't drink it,
but that means nothing to a man.
Mr. Hummel pours a saucer
on the porch steps,
but all it draws is flies.
"By God," he says, looking at us all,
"That dog is dumber than a pounded nail.
The best days that I've lived,
I've lived them wild and drunk."

6

The wine is deep in pickle crocks,
as gold as cider,
as cold as good well water.
You drink it from a dipper.

"Seems all I'd see
was pretty women in them days
when I was drinking hard stuff
on the river," Hummel says.
"Saw one, God's truth,
in Beavertown one time
that had a head of red hair
like a bonfire. And she was warm
in other spots."

We pass the dipper all around—
me, Jim Winland, Ealy Fishbeck,
and old Hummel, already shuffling cards.
"We'll play some euchre, boys,
then get another drink,
then we'll do the block and tackle."
"Block and tackle?" someone says.
"Yessir," Hummel says,
"You drink enough of that,
you walk a block
and tackle anything in sight."

7
Hours later,
and the sparrows
roosting in the eaves.
The trump invisible, the point-card
gone with oak-leaves in the breeze.

Jim Winland leans against a porch post,
Ealy Fishbeck wads a fresh chew,
loose as hay, fatter than a walnut,
and me and Mr. Hummel
pick the wood ticks off his hound.
"I've never seen no sense in ticks,
I'll tell you,"
Mr. Hummel says.
"Near everything I know
says ticks don't make
a bit of common sense.
Now even your tapeworm's
good for laughs, at least—
that cure that has a fellow
set his chin against the table
and then yawn,
and how that tapeworm
sashays out his mouth
to find that dish of milk
he set there—
but ticks!
By God,
they've beat me."

Ealy Fishbeck snorts,
and says,
"Hummel, life ain't all romance."

8
And then the moon hangs
like a ghost-fire
in the buckeye,

bats spin from the chimney,
and a big moth floats slow
above the white hood of the car.

Darkness. Everything you've seen
by day has brought the black suit
and gone home.

Silence.
Rustlings in the weeds.
Then, a flare of light
from down the porch:
Mr. Hummel stokes his apple pipe
and somehow, as you sit there,
smoke makes all the shapes
of creekbeds, blacksnakes,
of thrushy thickets
that the birdsong washes from
in rivers you can see,
and it is the best sight,
night-sight now,
the sweet wine climbing
to your eyes, and it is sleep, and all
the secret unspoiled places of your sleep
you want to float to,
down the rivers deep inside you,
slowly,
from this upland, weed-shored shack,
late at night,
in August,
in Ohio.

AUTUMN

1

Crossing light, long
shadows, ridgetops
gold: lily pods blazing
down road-edge, down
hardscrabble logging paths,
yellowed fern-verges.
In the woods, baubles
of persimmons, sweetening.
Down Brown's Run the creek
a narrow glinting of ingots,
the last dace brilliant
in the riffles,
a few goldfinches leaping
in broomsage, high over
on the high bank.
Day downing,
the green season
gone.

2

Often, this October,
I have thought of Mr. Whitacre's
story: a bucket
of coins,
buried in the hillside
behind his store—
a steep slope grading down
toward Clear Fork, Old Camp,

Cranesnest, all
directions.
Brag of fifty years,
the joke
this season deepens.

Now that ripening
of hoarded coins bursts
like seed.
The county washes aureate
at cold twilight:
gold-skinned heifer,
gilded fencepost,
groundhog.

Day downing,
the green season
gone,
prodigal autumn
spills free,
dazzles
every ridge.